PRESENT AFFAIRS

Angela Douglas

PRESENT AFFAIRS

Presents so beautiful
you can't bear to unwrap them

EBURY PRESS
LONDON

This book is for Kenny and my Father who both, in
their different ways, showed me how to give.

Published by Ebury Press
Division of The National Magazine Company Ltd
Colquhoun House
27—37 Broadwick Street
London W1V 1FR

First impression 1987

ISBN 0 85223 652 2

Editor: Gillian Haslam
Art Director: Frank Phillips
Designer: Roger Daniels
Photographer: Jon Bouchier
Illustrations: Hayward & Martin

Filmset by Advanced Filmsetters (Glasgow) Ltd

Printed and bound in Yugoslavia
by Mladinska knjiga, Ljubljana

CONTENTS

ACKNOWLEDGEMENTS

I would like to thank the following people for their help and enthusiasm while I worked on this book, especially my friend Beverley Holton, who was kind enough to be there when I needed her expertise, encouraging me through humour. I also greatly appreciate the special people at Ebury Press, Suzanne Webber, Frank Phillips and Gillian Haslam, for their moral support and creative involvement. Beyond that I want to thank Maria, who helps me take care of my house, for her patience and sweet temper, while I made such a chaotic mess of my kitchen, and for never once complaining about all the tedious cleaning up; to my literary agent, Vivienne Schuster for her shrewd advice and abundant encouragement; to my friends for understanding me; and to Felicity Green for helping, always. And to my Mother for her constant love.

THINGS YOU WILL NEED

Double-sided tape

Scissors—one large pair and one small pair

Florist wire

Millinery wire (black/white)

Small wire cutters

Stapler

Hole puncher

Metal ruler

Trimming knife

Clear varnish

Moulding clay

Small paint brush

Assorted buttons and beads

Needle and cotton

PENS

Black italic pen

Black felt tipped pen

Red felt tipped pen

Gold pen

Silver pen

Typist's correcting fluid

GLUES

Fabric glue

Paper glue

INTRODUCTION

*M*y Mother used to tell me, 'Don't ever say you won't do something, because as sure as birds will fly, you'll end up doing it every time'. Among the many varied and unexpected things I have done during my life, there was one thing I thought I'd never do—fancy gift wrapping. Both my Mother and my sister Elaine could make something beautiful out of almost anything, and for as long as I can remember Mummy was often to be seen at the kitchen table patiently sticking or snipping away, stopping now and again to see the effect from every angle until she'd achieved the look she wanted. I never once heard her say, 'Oh, that's good enough'. It had to be right.

When the house was filled with the hectic glow of Christmas, I was naturally expected to help. Ironing ribbons, making the stencils, spraying the fir cones ... all the simple tasks. As much as I would ooh and aah appreciatively at the often enchanting end results, I found it about as fascinating as watching a door warp! The preparations seemed to take forever. I am not a naturally patient person and I'd fidget, shifting from foot to foot, my small bosom heaving with boredom. I'd look at my Mother wearing my 'you'd forgive me anything' smile, but she'd fix me with a knowing glance, so I would say nothing about wanting another mince pie, or needing the loo—my mouth would just open and close like a fish. To make the time go faster I'd *try and count the loops on the bow she was making 5 ... 6 ... 7, and silently I'd promise myself that when I grew up I'd marry a posh man with a posh job so that I could buy everything I wanted from a posh shop. I'd smile at myself in the mirror over the fireplace, a sideways smile like actresses I'd seen in films, as I told myself I couldn't imagine wanting to learn to make anything, ever. How wrong can you be? I didn't appreciate it then, but I was learning by example the value and impact of a lovely present, and as I gradually discovered the very real delight of giving, I had to take it all back.*

Along the way I have learned lots of lessons. For instance, there are many ways of saving time and money without losing effect—you can use almost anything that might add interest to the colour, texture and shape. I've always been drawn to beautiful things and now my love of gift wrapping design is just a natural expression of that. I am an avid collector of practically everything—scraps of fabric, antique buttons, small silk flowers; at home I have a large pine military chest which belonged to my husband's grandfather and it's filled with boxes and cards, ribbons and paper; all sorts of useful odds and ends I've collected over the years. I hoard little scraps of this and that, so more often than not a speedy rummage will produce exactly the frippery I need.

People love presents, they offer different messages—bringing comfort to the ill, happiness to the lonely, reassurance of love and regard. That is what this book is all about. I've written it to encourage anyone who would like to develop their creative and frequently unawakened natural abilities—for those who love sparky new ideas. The ones I've given here are only a guide. Experiment—each person's sense of design is individual; substitute your favourite colour—I love yellow, you may not. Hopefully my approach will inspire you to be adventurous as I show you how it can be done, beautifully as well as simply. And to give you the confidence to believe that to wrap a present is easy—it works right away, for real beginners.

One final thought before you turn the page—my sister used to tell me, 'Angela—when you've discovered how to make something delightful, the real joy is in the sharing of it.' I think that's a sentiment that appeals to the friend in all of us.

Angela Douglas

WHERE DID YOU GET THAT HAT?

EASY. TAKES 30 MINUTES

I was on a bus earlier this year on one of those justifiably famous London Spring days—golden and warm, the parks massed with nodding daffodil and tulip blooms between great expanses of rich green lawns. An elderly woman sat in front of me wearing an enchanting hat of straw and ribbon and delicious silk flowers. It was obviously a much loved 'treasure' and as she left her seat she must have caught the admiration in my eyes and gave me the sweetest smile. I wished I had a Grandmother like her, and I decided to try and capture her hat in a design. This is for her and all Grandmothers.

SUGGESTED GIFTS

A book about famous English gardens

Box of Rose and Violet cream chocolates

Tea cup and saucer engraved 'To a very important person'

Magnifying glass with mother-of-pearl handle

YOU WILL NEED

Any shape of box

Half sheet of sweet-pea wrapping paper

Half paper doily

Mixed dried flowers—lavender, miniature roses and curry plant

Miniature basket

Miniature hat

Pale pink and lilac ribbon

Florist wire

Silver felt tipped pen

Double-sided tape

Scissors

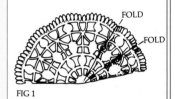

FOLD
FOLD
FIG 1

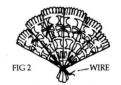

FIG 2 — WIRE

1 *Wrap box with tuck ends (see page 93).*

2 *Wire the flowers as a bunch, to lay flat on the box.*

3 *Pleat the doily into a loose fan shape (see figs 1 and 2).*

4 *Using double-sided tape place on the box, slightly off-centre. Place flowers on top and cover the stems with the small basket and hat.*

JINGLE ALL THE WAY

*T*his simple and traditional Christmas look is an old favourite of mine. My friends Charley and David ask for this design every year. If you fancy having a go, be sure to use three or four different kinds of ribbon of the same colour, as the idea is to mix the textures. The bells I've used came from a belt I wore back in the happy flower-power-love-your-brother days of the mid-60s!

SUGGESTED GIFTS

A box of 3 pairs of beautiful designer tights

A set of amusing magnets for the fridge door

A small brass money box

A travelling clock/radio

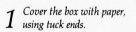

YOU WILL NEED

Any shape of box

Half sheet of red foil wrapping paper

10 bells, assorted sizes

Two different widths of red ribbon, 1 metre (40 in) in length

Curly ribbon

Florist wire

Double-sided tape

Scissors

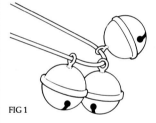

FIG 1

1 Cover the box with paper, using tuck ends.

2 Wire the jingle bells together with florist wire so that they look like two bunches of grapes. See fig 1.

3 Secure to the top of the box with double-sided tape, using a mass of whirly ribbon. Let it spill over the sides of the box.

4 Make ribbon bows, tying the centres with wire. See page 93.

5 Pile bows on to the top of the box, securing with double-sided tape.

WISHING YOU LOVE

*T*he wedding present is a splendid opportunity for you to be expressive and romantic. Last year friends who'd been invited to the wedding of Prince Andrew to Sarah Ferguson asked me to wrap their gift. It was an exciting undertaking, but I have to admit to a momentary attack of nerves—silly, isn't it!

YOU WILL NEED

Any shape of box

1 sheet of white flocked Japanese hand-made paper

Two 20 cm (8 in) white paper doilies

25 cm (10 in) white net

Needle and cotton

Assortment of crystal beads and pearls

White ribbon in three different widths, 50 cm (20 in) long

Small spray of white silk flowers

Scissors

Florist wire

Double-sided tape

Glue for paper

SUGGESTED GIFTS

Set of silver decanter labels

Small silver photograph frame, with a lucky four-leaf clover (cheat and make one up yourself!)

Six white linen table napkins embroidered with surname initial in white

Engraved Victorian silver sugar spoon

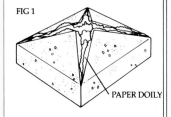

FIG 1

PAPER DOILY

FIG 2

1 Cover the top of the box with white paper, using double-sided tape.

2 Turn the box over and cover the bottom with enough paper overlapping to fold over and meet on the other side.

3 Place the doilies underneath the flaps so that the paper lace spills out underneath the flap. Stick the flaps down. See fig 1.

4 Gather the net with a needle and cotton and place over the flap join. Wire in the spray of silk flowers. See fig 2.

5 Make bows with ribbon and wire and stick into place. Glue beads and pearls on to the net and ribbons.

SUGAR AND SPICE

*S*ugar and spice and all things nice—I can't think of a more perfect theme for the birth of a baby girl. The rocky pink sugar sweets were a real find and they make an especially effective finish. But try and experiment with the many sweets available, and personalize the design with your own favourite. Can you see the tiny gold lettering on the ribbon? Perhaps a touch over the top but could anything look prettier?

YOU WILL NEED

Any shape of box

Half sheet of wrapping paper

Sweets, nutmeg, cinnamon sticks

50 cm (20 in) thin pink baby ribbon

Small scrap of pink satin

Sugar rock

Needle and cotton

Small transfer lettering
(size must fit width of baby ribbon)

Glue

Scissors

SUGGESTED GIFTS

Musical mobile for over the cot

Handmade patchwork quilt
for the cot

String of tiny seed pearls

Initialled silver spoon

1 Cover the box with wrapping paper, using tuck ends.

2 Make miniature bows from the satin, using a needle and cotton to secure.

3 Glue the sweets, nutmeg and cinnamon in a miniature pile on to the top of the box.

4 Add the bows and raw sugar.

5 Using the transfer lettering, write on to the ribbon 'Sugar and Spice and All Things Nice'. Arrange the ribbon on to the top of the box so that it curls around the pile of goodies.

WHO'S GOT THE KEY OF THE DOOR?

*T*wenty-first birthdays have their own personalities. Surely the recognition of a turning point in one's life deserves special treatment, and that treatment could be masses of flickering candles or clouds of high flying balloons. I've created the impression here of a front door—the glitter of the brass door knob and the ribbon with the tiny bunch of keys add an extra touch.

YOU WILL NEED

Oblong box

Red shiny card

Miniature door knocker/handle/letter box/keys
(you can make your own from card)

Gold transfer numbers

Trimming knife

Metal ruler

Black felt tipped pen

Double-sided tape

Scissors

Half sheet of brick paper

15 cm (6 in) thin red baby ribbon

1 Cover the box with the brick paper, using tuck ends.

2 Measure the front of the box, transfer the measurements on to the back of the red card, then cut the card carefully, using the knife and metal ruler.

3 Turn the card over and draw the panels of a Georgian door, using the black felt tipped pen and ruler. Position the numbers on to the door, then using double-sided tape stick the door into position.

4 Tie the miniature keys to the thin baby ribbon; stick the other end of the ribbon to the underside of the letter box, so that the keys appear to hang from the letter box.

SUGGESTED GIFTS

'Stay As Sweet As You Are' embroidered in white on a small white linen or cotton heart-shaped cushion

A small enamel birthday box engraved with the words 'The Best of Times is now'

Small silver carriage clock

Pair of earrings featuring the appropriate birthstone

MOTHER'S DAY SWEETIE BAG

*A*ll pink always looks lovely, particularly if you mix your materials. I hope she'll like this pretty coloured shop-bought bag; with a selection of sweets and a few bits and pieces you'll have all you need for this colourful treatment, when a simple box of chocolates doesn't seem special enough.

YOU WILL NEED

50 cm (20 in) pearlized cellophane

Assortment of sugar sweets
(not chocolate)

4 metres (4 yards) white whirly ribbon

Large pink shiny paper bag from a shop

Shredded tissue, pink

25 cm (10 in) pink net

Florist wire

Double-sided tape

Scissors

SUGGESTED GIFTS

Handmade pomander,
using tiny roses

Initialled note pad for
her bedside

Padded coat hangers

A gift token to spend at her
hairdresser

FIG 1

1 Stuff the bag with shredded tissue and insert the present.

2 Tie up the top of the bag to secure.

3 Wrap each sweet in cellophane and wire together, making a chain about 1½ metres long. See figs 1 and 2.

4 Loop over the bag, securing with wire.

5 Stick sweets haphazardly all over the top of the bag, using double-sided tape.

6 Wire through the net and curly ribbon and attach to the top of the bag, letting it spill down the sides of the bag.

FIG 2   WIRES

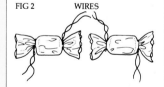

HEART-TO-HEART

DIFFICULT. TAKES 60 MINUTES

*S*t. Valentine's Day and hearts go together, and here are two, dressed up, plump in padded satin and presented in different ways. I enjoyed making them, and so should you, as they are an amusing way to express your sentiments to someone on a special occasion—or someone you'd like to make special.

YOU WILL NEED

Heart-shaped box

Heart-shaped cake board—I used 25 cm (10 in)

25 cm (10 in) quilting wadding

25 cm (10 in) red satin

25 cm (10 in) black satin

Double-sided tape and scissors

Glue for paper and fabric

Card for a heart-shaped template

RED HEART

15 cm (6 in) red ribbon, $1\frac{1}{4}$ cm ($\frac{1}{2}$ in) wide

60 cm (24 in) string of 6 mm ($\frac{1}{4}$ in) pearls, 250 individual ones

50 cm (20 in) spotted red/white ribbon, $1\frac{1}{4}$ cm ($\frac{1}{2}$ in) wide

One sheet of A4 paper

One sheet of red shiny wrapping paper

Miniature gold transfer lettering

BLACK HEART

25 cm (10 in) of black flock paper

3 shiny buttons

Small chocolate coins for medals

One sheet of black shiny paper

5 cm (2 in) black velvet ribbon, 6 mm ($\frac{1}{4}$ in) wide, for bow tie

1 Cover box with shiny paper, using tuck ends.

2 Cover one side of the cake board with paper glue. Stick on the wadding, trim surplus.

3 Turn over the cake board and again cover with paper glue, covering the edges.

4 Lay out the satin with the shiny side down, place the wadding side of the heart down in the centre of the fabric.

5 Working around the heart pull the satin over, sticking and pleating as you go, making sure you pull the fabric taut, pulling out the creases before sticking down on the underside.

6 Using double-sided tape and the red ribbon, cover the outside edge to hide any bumps and to give a neat edge.

RED HEART

Glue the pearls around the edge. Draw two heart shapes on the card and cut out—one is to make template and the other is for the bottom of the heart-shaped hole. Using the transfer lettering, write the message on to the first card heart. Use the template heart placed in the centre of the big satin heart to draw around and cut out with a trimming knife. Cover the template in satin—this is the door to cover the hole. Line the hole with ribbon, place the message heart in the bottom of the hole, hinge the door with ribbon, surround with pearls, fixing with glue. Make a bow with spotted ribbon and place at the top of the heart. Place the whole heart on to the shiny paper box.

BLACK HEART

Cover as above using black satin. Make a V-shaped shirt front from white card. Use the flock paper to make velvet lapels. Glue on the medals, make a small bow tie and stick at the top. Stick the buttons down the front.

SUGGESTED GIFTS

A genuine Victorian Valentine

A cushion embroidered 'Come Live with Me and Be My Love'

A heart-shaped brooch engraved with 'I'm With You'

Ice tray for heart-shaped cubes

Bloomin' Lovely

*A*s moss and fresh flowers complement each other so naturally, this makes a delightful wedding gift. I first used the idea for friends who had a country wedding last year, and I was careful to choose flowers that wouldn't wilt within a couple of hours of being picked. Before arranging them I filled the Victorian silver sugar shaker I'd bought them with multi-coloured chocolate beans and masses of minute silver stars. With all the time and thought that went into this present went my good wishes.

YOU WILL NEED

One wicker basket, size depending on present

Large selection of white flowers

White whirly ribbon

Shredded white tissue

2 pieces dampened florist's foam

Plastic dish

SUGGESTED GIFTS

A pair of Lalique crystal champagne glasses

A small white linen pillow embroidered with the words 'The Best Is Yet to Come'

Sterling silver desk calendar

Ice-cream making machine

1 Lay the shredded tissue in the bottom of the basket, nestle the gift in the tissue, cover with cling film to protect it.

2 Put the dampened foam into a plastic dish which will fit into the basket. Lower into basket, arrange flowers in a mass, spilling out over the edges, filling the basket.

3 Attach the whirly ribbon to the base of the handle of the basket on each side.

EAT YOUR HEART OUT

I am a secret eater! I love sitting in front of the T.V. with nothing but a box of sweets between me and the rest of the world! Yet I foolishly wonder why, when I look in the mirror, all I see are apple cheeks and thunder thighs! 'I'm all circles' is a frequent and pathetic plea I make to my stepdaughter Jane. She looks at me, 'You're not fat, Angela, very definitely not fat.' I've always trusted my friends, so this one is for me!

YOU WILL NEED

A large assortment of sweets

Mini chocolate bars

Candy sticks

Any shape of box

25 cm (10 in) cellophane

Clear varnish and paint brush

Glue for paper

Cellophane angel hair

Thin strands of cellophane or pearlized whirly ribbon

Half sheet of silver paper

50 cm (20 in) of pink net

Double-sided tape

Florist wire

1 Cover the box with silver paper.

2 Varnish the chocolate bars and leave to dry.

3 Pile on the chocolate bars and sweets, building a mountain in the centre of box. Glue into place.

4 Make small bows with wire and frill the fru fru net. Place them haphazardly all over the sweet mountain.

5 Shake the stranded cellophane all over the finished box.

SUGGESTED GIFTS

Edwardian style ceramic kitchen storage jars

At Home and Abroad leather address books

Travelling felt shoe bags

Earthenware jug inscribed 'A present for a friend'

SCHOOL'S OUT FOR EVER

*P*eople who enjoyed their school days have no sympathy whatever with we 'dummies' who didn't! I was full of dread and fear just entering the playground. I remember one teacher who looked like a big grey cat actually throwing an egg at me when he caught me passing rude notes to the girl behind me. When I walked out of the school gates for the last time I thought 'Yippee, this is life . . . living!'.

YOU WILL NEED

Oblong box

Wood grain paper

Sugar paper, black

Different colours of chalk

Double-sided tape

Scissors

1 Cover one flat side of the box with the black sugar paper, using double-sided tape.

2 Cover the other flat side using the wood grain paper, again using the double-sided tape. Cover the edges of the box with wood grain paper and double-sided tape.

3 Using the chalk, draw the message on to the black sugar paper. Stick two or three chalks on the left hand corner of the blackboard using double-sided tape.

SUGGESTED GIFTS

A little dried flower bouquet

A tin of home-made and sinful chocolate cake

Cotton sponge bag and matching make-up purse

Liberty-print covered address book

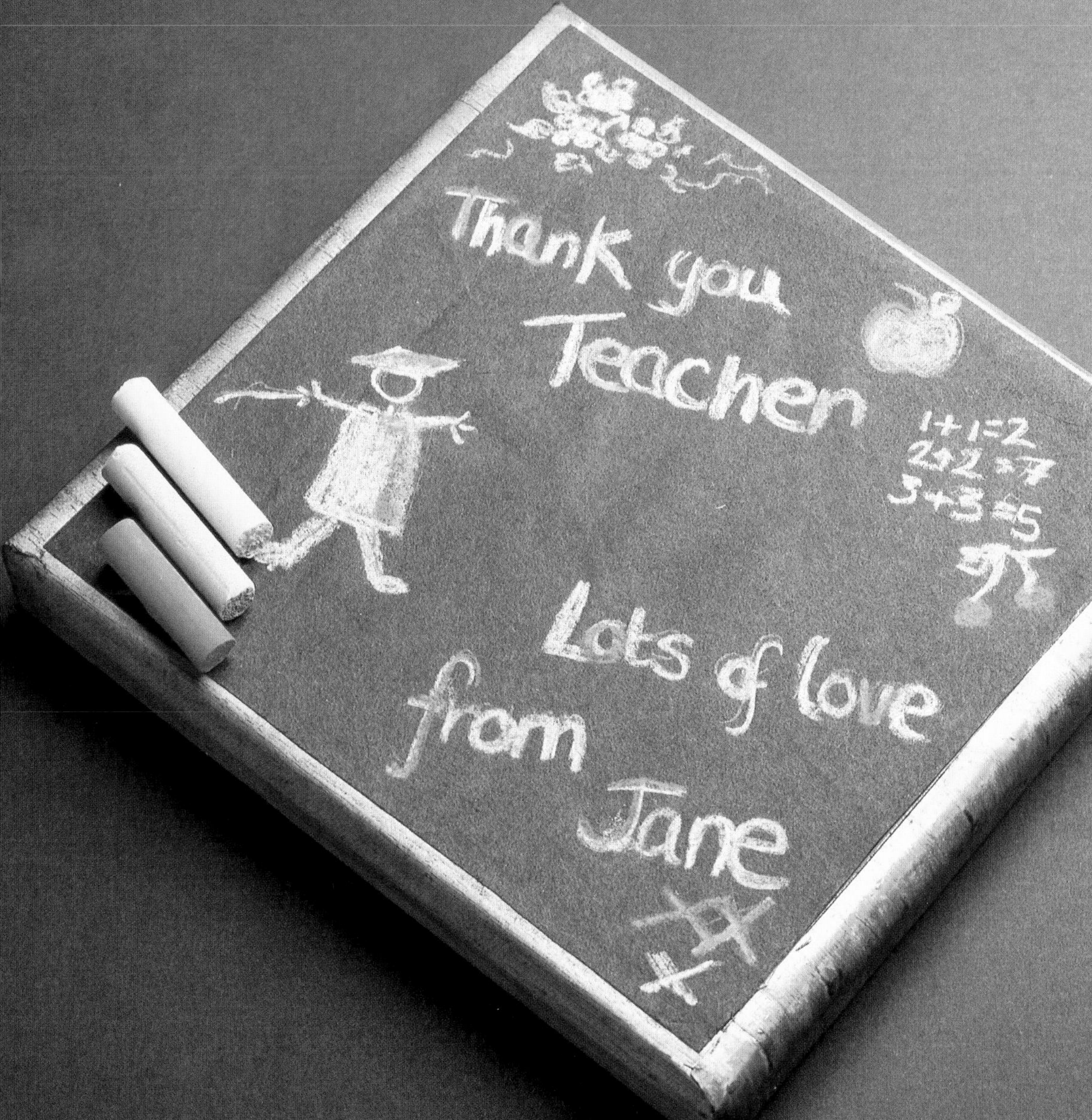
Thank you
Teacher
1+1=2
Lots of love
from
Jane

LOOKS LIKE LOVE

I loved making this pink fru-fru wedding present and it was deceptively simple. I chose a pink theme, rather than the traditional white, because it was second time around for both bride and groom. You could use any shape of box and with different colour schemes it would look pretty for various special occasions.

SUGGESTED GIFTS

Set of six French dessert plates

Needlepoint cushion embroidered with the words 'Just For You'

Set of monogrammed silver napkin rings

Pair of crystal goblets engraved with initials

YOU WILL NEED

Any shape of box

Wrapping paper, marbled pink

Scissors

Double-sided tape

Florist wire

Contrasting crepe paper, 2 different colours

1 metre (40 in) pleated tulle or ballet net

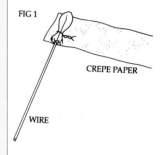

FIG 1

CREPE PAPER

WIRE

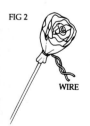

FIG 2

WIRE

1 Cover box in wrapping paper (see page 92).

2 Cut crepe paper in 2·5 cm (1 in) wide strips; pull each strip to stretch out the creases.

3 Cut off 4 cm (1½ in) to make the bud (see fig 1).

4 Roll this around the top of one stem of florist wire.

5 Holding wire in one band, roll the long strip of crepe paper around the bud, to look like a rose (see fig 2).

6 Secure the end of the papers with wire. Bend back the petals a little to give full effect of a flower.

7 Make 14 rose heads in this way.

8 Cut tulle into six circles, 30 cm (12 in) diameter; use a dinner plate as a template.

9 Lay circles on top of each other, push wire through the centre and secure to the centre of the box.

10 Arrange the flowers in the folds of the net; secure them with double-sided tape and by twisting the wire.

11 Cut off all loose ends of wire with cutters.

BETTER LATE THAN NEVER

*M*y obsession, honestly, is punctuality. I go pink and shiny at the very thought of keeping somebody waiting, and I can tell myself until I'm dizzy that I don't mind people being late for me, but I do, I do! So this design is for a dear girl friend, highly successful in the designing business, who drives me crazy. I swear she'll be late for her own funeral! My husband used to tell me 'Never carry a grudge, darling. While you're carrying the grudge they're out dancing.' I agree with that.

SUGGESTED GIFTS

Small enamel pill box marked with the year

Initialled moiré sachet filled with lavender

Aromatic burning oil with light bulb ring

Two pairs of fun socks

YOU WILL NEED

Round box

Quarter sheet of white paper

Double-sided tape and scissors

Stick-on numerals

8 large gold jingle bells

50 cm (20 in) ribbon, 1 cm (½in) wide

Strip of gold paper, 2·5 cm (1 in) wide

Ribbon

Adhesive plasticine

1 Cover round box with white paper, as shown on page 92.

2 Stick a band of gold paper around the top rim of box. See fig 1.

3 Using a ruler and pencil, mark the 'face' of the clock into quarters—this helps you to keep the numerals in the correct position. See fig 2.

4 Stick the numbers on to the 'face'.

5 Using gold paper backed with double-sided tape cut out two arms, one longer than the other. Place on the 'face' of the clock.

6 Using two bells to make the feet of the clock, stick on the bottom of the box with double-sided tape and adhesive plasticine.

7 Cluster six bells on the top of the clock with double-sided tape and ribbon.

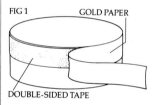

FIG 1   GOLD PAPER

DOUBLE-SIDED TAPE

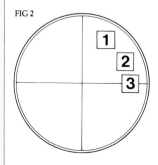

FIG 2

BIRTHDAY BABY

*T*he first birthday of a baby is very special, isn't it? I made this for my adorable little god-daughter, Harriet, and I liked the idea of trying to reproduce her birthday cake as her present. It gave me so much pleasure to watch the little one's reaction. There were smiles all round.

SUGGESTED GIFTS

As large a fluffy teddy-bear as you can find

Some Premium Bonds

A home video recording of the day's events

Fairy tale picture featuring the child's name

YOU WILL NEED

Round box

Half sheet of pink wrapping paper

Crepe paper

Double-sided tape

Scissors

Birthday candle

Whirly ribbon — pink

Cake board 4 cm ($1\frac{1}{2}$ in) larger than the box

Sugar letter-sweets

White paper doily

Glue for paper

1 Cover the top of the box with paper, sticking with double-sided tape. Cut off surplus.

2 Cut crepe paper to act as cake frill, the same as the depth of the box.

3 Snip a little frill, do the same with another strip of crepe which is narrower by 2·5 cm (1 in). Stick around the outside of the box with tape.

4 Tie white ribbon around the edge and tie bow, place flowers in centre.

5 Pierce a hole into the top of the box, push in a mass of curly ribbon and the candle.

6 Put the white doily on to the cake board, stick 'cake' on to the board with double-sided tape. Add curls of whirly ribbon around the edge. Glue the sugar sweets so that they read 'Baby's 1st'.

7 Make a gift card from the paper and place underneath mass of ribbons on top of the lid.

HERE'S LOOKING AT YOU

*H*ere is my version of a theatre dressing table mirror. I first made this for my husband several Christmases ago when he was appearing at the Savoy Theatre. It's almost a tradition that when one vacates a dressing room, a message of good luck is scrawled in lipstick on the mirror for the next occupant. Lipstick doesn't work very well on this silver paper so I used nail varnish, but was a bit heavy handed on the M. Sorry!

YOU WILL NEED

Oblong box

Mirror paper

25 cm (10 in) red ribbon, 1·25 cm ($\frac{1}{2}$in) wide

A sprig of holly or a plastic equivalent

Nail varnish pen in red

Small Christmas baubles, preferably plastic

Double-sided tape

Scissors

Glue for paper

SUGGESTED GIFTS

A theatrical biography

An original copy of The Times newspaper, date and year of birth

A video of a favourite film

Knit a special cushion for a desk chair

1 Cover the box with mirror paper, using flap ends.

2 Use a nail varnish pen to write out the message and leave to dry.

3 Pierce holes using tip of scissors or a kitchen skewer about 1 cm ($\frac{1}{2}$in) in from the edge of the box. You almost have to screw in the baubles as if they were real light bulbs. If necessary use a small amount of glue to secure.

4 Tie the red ribbon around the holly sprig and place in the bottom left hand corner of the box. Secure with double-sided tape.

OUT FOR TEA WITH NANETTE

*T*he happy hours I've spent with Nanette and Bryan Forbes were very much in my mind as I worked on this gift for them. It's not simply this pretty box that is important, as much as my warm thoughts of their supportive friendship which add to my happiness.

YOU WILL NEED

Any shape of box

One sheet of wrapping paper to cover box

One sheet of wrapping paper with small floral design

Miniature tea set

Miniature food/basket of flowers/egg basket

1 paper doily

Scissors

Double-sided tape

SUGGESTED GIFTS

Cut glass inkwells with silver lids

Wool and silk shawl

Burr maple photograph frame

Mixed box of herbal teas

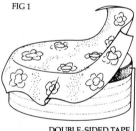

FIG 1

DOUBLE-SIDED TAPE

1 Cover the box around the edges—it does not matter if you overlap at the top and the bottom, both will be hidden.

2 Cut a square of paper to make a tablecloth. Cover the top of the box with double-sided tape, peel off backing and place cloth over table, pleating into soft folds, securing where necessary with tape, cutting off surplus. See fig 1.

3 Using double-sided tape stick a doily over the top to look like a lace cloth.

4 With double-sided tape secure the miniatures into place on the top of the tea table.

LITTLE BOY BLUE

*F*or any important occasion I try to make my gift look special, and particularly perhaps for a christening. My girl friend Veronica showed me how to make this colourful and thoroughly charming cushion cover and I was so thrilled with the way it turned out that I could hardly bear to part with it! If it's for a little girl then naturally the blue wool should be replaced by pink. With appropriate wording it could cover several occasions—Thank You, Get Well Soon—a light and amusing way to get any message across.

YOU WILL NEED

For the knitted cushion cover:

Two 50 g (2 oz) balls of 4-ply wool

Size 11 needles

Four different coloured oddments of wool

Embroidery needle

One feather cushion pad 36 cm × 36 cm (14 in × 14 in)

1 *Knit one long piece 36 cm (14 in) wide and 75 cm (30 in) long. You can use any sort of pattern you wish, depending on your knitting skills. Take into account that the length is folded to make a cushion with the two edges meeting at the back and securing with press studs.*

2 *Swiss embroider (oversew) the following information on to the front of the cushion using the oddments—the name of the child, date and time of birth, colour of hair, eyes, weight at birth, and the birth sign.*

3 *Stuff with a feather cushion. Slip the gift inside if it is something small.*

SUGGESTED GIFTS

Small initialled white leather prayer book

Silver hairbrush with engraved initials

Personalized pencil box painted with Beatrix Potter figures

Some wine laid down

BOTTLES WITH A BANG!

MEDIUM EASY. TAKES 40 MINUTES

I've heard friends groan while trying to wrap a bottle of wine 'Oh, please do it for me, Angela', but it really isn't that difficult and like everything else it's easy once you know how. I did the red Christmas one for my bank manager, who luckily also happens to be a friend and the silver for my god-son's eighteenth birthday. As I finished it I realized how effective it would look done in yellows for Easter, pinks for the birth of a baby girl, greens for St. Patrick's Day . . . and on and on and on . . .

YOU WILL NEED

1 bottle bag

Shredded tissue paper

Ribbon

Florist wire

Double-sided tape

Red felt tipped pen

One cheque

Sequin waste

1 To shred tissue paper, follow instructions on page 93.

2 To make bows, follow instructions on page 93.

3 Staple sequin waste bow to the bag, then the cheque to the bow. Attach the curly ribbon with double-sided tape.

VARIATION
For the silver wrapping, roll a sheet of silver paper around the bottle. Secure at the neck of the bottle with gold ribbon. Fill the open top with masses of gold ribbon with fish tailed ends.

SUGGESTED GIFTS

Bottle of champagne

Bottle of home-made raspberry vinegar

Bottle of stem ginger

Bottle of first pressing of olive oil

MERRY CHRISTMAS LOVE AND KISSES

Yes, it's supposed to be sexy so don't panic! I love it, you may not, since to wrap a Christmas gift in shiny black paper and frilly garter is a break with tradition—if you've a real garter tucked away, why not use that. It's always enjoyable to bring some fun into a gift.

YOU WILL NEED

Any shape of box

Half sheet of black wrapping paper

1·5 metres (60 in) black sequin waste

Double-sided tape

Scissors

Two small bells

50 cm (20 in) lace, 5 cm (2 in) wide

50 cm (20 in) black grosgrain ribbon

Gold marking pen

Needle and black cotton

SUGGESTED GIFTS

Pair of leather driving gloves

Stripey red/white/black cotton boxer shorts

A pair of Victorian grape scissors

Aftershave and matching shower gel

1 Wrap box, using flap ends, with black wrapping paper.

2 Using double-sided tape, cover the box with the sequin waste by wrapping it around lengthways, taking it back on itself and trimming.

3 Gather the lace with a needle and cotton, making sure that it will be taken across the top of the box, widthways. Let the lace lap over the edges.

4 Write the message on to the length of ribbon and secure over the lace with double-sided tape.

5 Make a bow and sew in the centre two bells.

6 Attach the bow to the far left hand corner of the garter with double-sided tape.

FOR DARLING DADDY ON HIS SPECIAL DAY

We all think we have the best Dad in the world and I originally made this years ago for mine, using the Sporting Life as the wrapping paper, a pile of fun paper money and a jockey's cap in his favourite colours, as he'd been known to have a flutter or two on the horses! I did this particular one for the stockbroker father of a friend of mine, using a trio of his favourite things—the Financial Times, cigarettes and his bow-tie, and the little bottle of brandy gets all dressed up!

YOU WILL NEED

Any shape of box

Double-sided tape

Scissors

String

Luggage label

Black felt tipped pen

Financial Times or other newspaper

Miniature bottle of brandy

2 cigarette pencils

Bow tie, or fabric to make one

1 Cover the box using tuck ends method.

2 Tie string as you would on a brown parcel.

3 Using double-sided tape, stick the miniature bottle and cigarette pencils on to one crossing of the parcel string.

4 Attach bow tie to neck of bottle. If you have to make a bow tie, use the method for making a big bow shown on page 93, using a piece of fabric 10 × 25 cm (4 × 10 in).

SUGGESTED GIFTS

Copy of Roget's International Thesaurus

Silk tie with co-ordinating handkerchief

Glass Perthshire paperweights

Silver pill box

Darling Daddy
REMY MARTIN
FINANCIAL
Tuesday
Wapping inquiry call
Pincer

AUSTRALIA'S SUNSHINE DAY

*A*lthough I admit to having dozed off at many a cricket match, this gift is one of my favourites—it's very simple but looks immediately Australian and the little bear belongs to Frank Phillips, art director on this book. He's a much loved bear and I can see why—he looks so willing to please, holding on to his piece of eucalyptus and national flag. I've never been to Australia but long to. Maybe one day . . .

YOU WILL NEED

Any shape of box

50 cm (20 in) green velour paper

Double-sided tape

Scissors

Miniature cricket set*

Small koala bear

Eucalyptus stem

Paper Australian flag on a cocktail stick

*If you're good at modelling things in miniature, you could make the cricket bats, stumps and ball. As I was busy rehearsing a play, I cheated and bought these.

1 Cover the box with velour paper, using tuck ends (see page 93).

2 Set up wickets and bats and keep in place with double-sided tape.

3 Stick the koala on to the box, making him hold the miniature flag and eucalyptus stem.

SUGGESTED GIFTS

Coloured canvas bag for the beach

Pair of yachting shoes

Torch magnifying glass

A pair of folding sunglasses

CHRISTMAS SACK OF SWEET SURPRISES

MEDIUM EASY, IF YOU CAN KNIT

*C*hristmas comes but once a year, and it's a very special time for children. They look forward to it for weeks, talking of little else, and the joyous memories of early childhood will last a lifetime. With its glowing reds and greens this sack will surely dazzle and be the star under any Christmas tree.

YOU WILL NEED

Two 50 g (2 oz) balls of 4-ply wool

Size 11 needles

4 different coloured oddments for embroidery

Embroidery needle

50 cm (20 in) cord for the drawstring

2 small bells

SACK FILLING

Red shredded tissue paper

Red/green shiny wrapping paper

Red/green whirly ribbon

Assorted small gifts

SUGGESTED GIFTS

Small stuffed toy animals or dolls

Miniature phials of bath essence and soap

Fun bracelets and watches

Coloured pencils, coloured candy

1 Knit two squares using stocking stitch, 36 cm × 36 cm (14 in × 14 in). You could use a fairisle pattern border as I have or you could use your own design. I have used Swiss embroidery (oversewing) for the lettering after the square has been knitted.

2 Sew up the three seams, turning the sack inside out so that the seams are hidden.

3 Thread through the cord about 2·5 cm (1 in) down from the top of the sack—this is the drawstring. Tie a little bell on each end of the cord.

4 Stuff the sack with shredded tissue, wrap the small presents in the shiny paper, using the contrasting whirly ribbon and arrange the presents in the sack so they appear to be spilling out.

ALL THAT GLITTERS

*T*his makes a really glamorous looking gift. I made it for our great friends Harry and Nellie Bryan. I hadn't been working much, money was slippery and I thought 'Golden Wedding, ouch!'. But actually I didn't spend lots on their gift, some chocolates covered in gold foil, and I needlepointed a cushion with 'Good As Gold'. They were thrilled. And next time I'll try not to eat so many chocolates . . .

SUGGESTED GIFTS

Small crystal heart-shaped box with gilt bow and filled with gold dragées

Gold toothbrush and a tube of champagne flavoured toothpaste

Forty 'Soleil d'Or' daffodil bulbs

Tape of the 'Golden Years' of Bing Crosby

YOU WILL NEED

Any shape of box

Sheet of gold foil paper

Double-sided tape and scissors

2 metres (80 in) gold foil curly ribbon

60 cm (24 in) gold sequin waste

Gold card for gift tag

Gold corrugated paper

Gold chocolate coins

Gold felt tipped pen

2 different ribbons, 60 cm (24 in) long

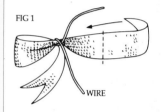

FIG 1

WIRE

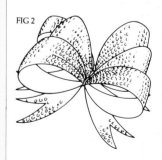

FIG 2

1 Cover box as shown on page 92.

2 Hold the sequin waste in a bow and tie wire around centre to fasten (fig 1).

3 Wire the two ribbons into bows in the same way.

4 Wire all three together, cut ends of wire leaving one to fasten to box. See fig 2. Fish tail ends of ribbon and tape in position.

5 Tie six lengths of whirly ribbon together and curl using whirly method on page 93.

6 Edge the circumference of the box with the gold corrugated paper using double-sided tape.

7 Fold the gift card and write in it. Tape on the box underneath ribbon mass.

8 Tape coins as if scattered over box.

OFF THE WALL

*U*ntil now I've never taken much notice of graffiti except to think what a nuisance it must be to have one's walls spoiled and what hard work it must be to clean off. When I wanted to make this for my nephew Joe on his last birthday, I found it difficult to think of appropriate slang slogans to write over the paper as I didn't know who the top football teams were or the favourite pop stars. So I asked his elder brother James to help me. He had some very good ideas—here are a few of the less sensational!

YOU WILL NEED

Any shape of box

Slate doll's house paper

Double-sided tape

Scissors

An assortment of felt tipped pens

Typist's correcting fluid

SUGGESTED GIFTS

Cotton towelling robe

Computer game

Swiss army knife

Matt black fountain pen

1 *Cover the box with paper, using tuck ends (see page 93).*

2 *Draw and scribble anything and everything which is relevant to the person and the occasion. The correcting fluid gives the effect of white paint.*

SHORTHAND SURPRISE

*W*hy not make your secretary feel special and appreciated, especially as this must be one of the quickest gifts in the book? Don't worry if you can't find a pencil with her name on it, a plain one would do—it's just an added detail. Of course you can write something suitable to fit any occasion on the note pad.

YOU WILL NEED

Oblong box

Half sheet of wrapping paper, pink parchment

Personalized pencil, monogrammed

Pastel coloured spiral bound notebook

Black italic pen

Whirly ribbon—ten lengths of 50 cm (20 in)

Double-sided tape

Scissors

SUGGESTED GIFTS

Gift token for a day at a health farm

Leather diary with note pad and pen

Travelling cassette holder

A generously sized leather shoulder bag

FIG 1

CURL TOP PAGE

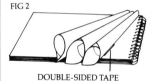

FIG 2

DOUBLE-SIDED TAPE

1 Cover the box with paper, using flap ends.

2 Place the notebook at a slight angle on the box, using double-sided tape to secure.

3 Tie the ten strands of whirly ribbon on to the spiral of the notebook.

4 Curl and fold back the pages of the notebook (see fig 1). Secure with tape. (see fig 2).

5 Write a message on the last exposed page, using double-sided tape again to secure the pencil across the page.

THANKS TO YOU

I admit to being sentimental, treasuring the gifts given to me through the years by my family and friends. If I had to make a list of my most favourite, then this little clay bear made specially for me by the gifted Margaret Ballard would surely be close to the top. Of course I wouldn't dream of parting with it and have only used it here to give you the idea that almost anything may be used as a centre decoration—tassels, toys, buttons, bows, candy, candles ... got the idea? There are no rules, just let your imagination go!

<u>SUGGESTED GIFTS</u>

A book on dried flower arranging

Automatic coffee machine

Classic cashmere cardigan

Traditional Provençal design cotton cushion for the garden

YOU WILL NEED

Any shape of box

Quarter sheet of paper—doll's house wallpaper

Moiré ribbon. 6·25 cm (2½ in) wide

Double-sided tape

Scissors

1 Cover the box, as shown on page 92.

2 Using double-sided tape all around the rim of the box, peel off the backing and put to one side.

3 Catch the ribbon in three places with a needle and cotton (see fig 1), then stick to the exposed tape on the rim of the box (see fig 2). Using a thinner ribbon and double-sided tape, cover the gathering stitches.

4 Using double-sided tape cover the base of the teddy-bear, curl strips of the paper with scissors as you do with the ribbon on page 93 and stick to the underside of the teddy base.

5 Again using the double-sided tape, place the teddy-bear in the centre of the box.

FIG 1

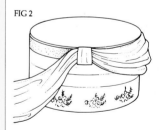

FIG 2

EASTER BASKET BREEZE

*T*here's everything about this bright and abundant basket that speaks to us with all the accents of Spring. Once the gift which is hidden under the straw has been retrieved and when all the tiny chocolate eggs have been eaten (just watch them disappear!) there is a lovely basket to keep—the best of both worlds.

SUGGESTED GIFTS

Set of pretty initialled egg cups, one for each member of the family

A seersucker hanging tidy, perfect for gloves, belts, tights

Pretty mini-patchwork egg cosies

A Victorian silver sweet basket, filled with home-made chocolate bunnies (and you'd better make plenty!)

YOU WILL NEED

Six eggs

Poster paint in pastel colours

Straw

Two bunches of grasses—different colours and types

Round basket

Clear varnish

Sugar Easter eggs

Paint brush

Wire

Wire cutters

Glue for paper

Hot Cross buns/small grained bread rolls

1 metre (40 in) yellow dotted ribbon, 1·25 cm ($\frac{1}{2}$in) wide

1 metre (40 in) yellow ribbon, 2·5 cm (1 in) wide

1 Split the grasses into small bunches, trimming the stems with wire clockwise around the rim of the basket, alternating the grasses.

2 Paint the real eggs with the pastel water colours, varnish and leave to dry.

3 Cut the hot cross buns and bread rolls in half and wire to the grasses—varnish and leave to dry.

4 Make small bows and secure with wire to the grasses.

5 Stick with glue the sugar coated chocolate eggs dotting them all around the rim.

6 Fill the basket with straw and the stems of the grasses; to hide the gift make a nest on the top and nestle the eggs in the straw.

THE FLAVOUR OF CHRISTMAS

'*You're a smashing cook, Auntie' my nephews Joe and James said when I made their favourite cinnamon cake. Well, I'm not really but that compliment was enough to inspire this design. I like to try and use a theme relevant to the person and I thought to use sections of cinnamon sticks as decoration might be unusual. Your message on the gift card scroll should be written in red.*

SUGGESTED GIFTS

Glass scent bottle with engraved
name

Simulated lizard belt with
interchangeable buckles

Leather telephone jotter with
initials

Seersucker lined sewing basket

YOU WILL NEED

Any shape of box

Half sheet of red foil paper

2 cinnamon sticks

Double-sided tape and scissors

3 types of brown ribbon, each 20 cm (8 in)

1 short piece of red ribbon

1 tiny piece of parchment paper for the gift card

Can of gold spray paint and red felt tipped pen

Can of gold spray paint

1 strip of gold/green fine tinsel

Millinery/florist wire

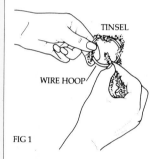

TINSEL

WIRE HOOP

FIG 1

FIG 2

WIRING CONES AND BERRIES

1 Spray some of the berries and all the fir cones liberally with the gold paint and leave to dry.

2 Cover the box with foil paper, using tuck ends.

3 Cut cinnamon into 3 cm (1¼in) pieces. Tie a bow around centre, using different ribbons.

4 Make one wire ring, 4·5 cm (1¾in) diameter. Twist the tinsel around the ring. See fig 1.

5 Wire the berries together on to the hoop, interspaced with fir cones. See fig 2.

6 Cover the bottom with double-sided tape and place on box, off centre, to one corner.

7 Place the cinnamon sticks into the hole in the centre.

8 For the gift tag cut a rectangle of parchment paper and roll into miniature scroll, then tie with red ribbon.

COTTON PICKING PRETTY

*I*bought this fabric some time ago without having any idea what I would use it for. An impulse buy if you like, but it was so pretty I knew it would come in useful for something, and I tucked it away in my old pine chest. When I started searching for ideas for this book, I came across it and remembered that the first wedding anniversary gift is traditionally cotton. I used the border from the fabric to make the bows, and was pleased with the way it turned out—very fresh, very colourful.

SUGGESTED GIFTS

Pot of Herbes de Provence

Subscription to a favourite magazine

Set of new kitchen knives

Olive wood salad bowl from Provence

YOU WILL NEED

Any shape of box

50 cm (20 in) of fabric

1 metre (40 in) of border to match

Double-sided tape

Scissors

Needle and thread

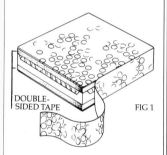

DOUBLE-SIDED TAPE   FIG 1

1   *Iron the fabric before using, to remove all the creases.*

2   *Cover the top of the box with a piece of the fabric, using the double-sided tape along all four sides of the box.*

3   *Stick the tape around the rim of the box.*

4   *Peel off backing, and stick a strip of fabric around the edge. See fig 1.*

5   *Treat the fabric border as if it was ribbon and place a strip backed with double-sided tape horizontally down the side of the box, using the rest to make two small compact bows. Fold the material in half, and cover the join with a small piece of fabric. Stitch in place.*

6   *Place on the box, using double-sided tape. See fig 2.*

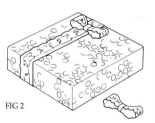

FIG 2

THANKSGIVING IN THE USA

I was unfamiliar with the historical origins of America's Thanksgiving celebrations until I was told about the seventeenth century Pilgrim Fathers holding a religious service to thank God for a particularly plentiful harvest. So it was easy to choose this design as you can't get more rural than a bunch of glowingly ripe corn or more patriotic than the Stars and Stripes flag!

YOU WILL NEED

Any shape of box

A bunch of dried corn

Two cocktail flags

1 metre (40 in) gardener's twine

1 sheet of parchment wrapping paper

Double-sided tape

Florist wire

Scissors

1 Cover the box with paper, using tuck ends.

2 Bind the grasses together with wire, and cover the wire with plaited garden twine.

3 Cut the stems of the dried corn so that they are in proportion to the box, and stick to the box with double-sided tape.

4 Stick the USA cocktail flags into the bunch of corn.

SUGGESTED GIFTS

Prettily decorated tin filled with home-made cookies

A book showing Remington's famous Red Indian paintings

A bottle of Californian champagne

Two pretty pure cotton hand towels

HAT TRICK

*T*here's something about yellow—zingy, fresh and sparkling that reminds us of Spring. This is a delicious and sophisticated look, perfect for a lady who loves hats. Try it in any colour. I know this might look like an all evening effort, but it isn't. Although full of detail this is really very easy.

YOU WILL NEED

Round box

Half a sheet of yellow paper

Needle and cotton

15 cm (6 in) of hat net

Curly white ribbon

Two 50 cm (20 in) lengths of white ribbon

50 cm (20 in) yellow ribbon, 1 cm ($\frac{1}{2}$ in) wide

Double-sided tape and scissors

Pearly buttons and glue for paper

SUGGESTED GIFTS

Small black satin evening bag

A botanical print in maple frame

Round box of pot-pourri

Classic cream silk shirt

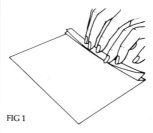

FIG 1

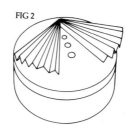

FIG 2

1 Cover round box using the method on page 92.

2 Stick double-sided tape to the back of one strip of white ribbon. Peel off paper and stick around the rim of the box.

3 Make bows out of the other two lengths of ribbon, as shown on page 93.

4 Tape the yellow bow on to the top of the box.

5 Place white bow on to the back of 'hat'—tie in about 8 lengths of curly ribbon which hangs over the edge of the box.

6 Make a paper fan with a square of yellow paper, folding it every 1 cm ($\frac{1}{2}$ in) to give a concertina effect. See fig 1.

7 Fold fan in half lengthways and place on top of the box with double-sided tape. See fig 2.

8 Glue the three buttons in a line down the centre.

9 Gather the hat net with a needle and cotton along one side, tape underneath yellow bow.

10 Fish tail all the ends of the bows.

BON VOYAGE

*T*he principle behind each gift is the same; the desire to please someone you care about in a personal way. The delightful thing about this little suitcase is that whatever you decide to use as a decoration, you can be versatile. It's a good opportunity to use all your favourite slogans—or make some up! Remember to cut your stickers to scale and don't forget to write your favourite address in the little label.

YOU WILL NEED

Oblong box

Blue leatherette wrapping paper

Travelling labels/stickers

Double-sided tape and scissors

Three buckles, 4 cm (1$\frac{1}{2}$in) wide

Silver foil/mirror paper, 4 squares

1 Cover the box with wrapping paper, using tuck ends.

2 Fold a strip of wrapping paper into a strip of about 4 cm (1$\frac{1}{2}$in) wide. Cut to a 18 cm (7 in) length—this is to make the handle of the suitcase.

3 Stick double-sided tape on each end of the strip and place on to the top of the box, making sure it is equally positioned.

4 Cut two more lengths off the strip, about 7·5 cm (3 in) long; point the ends to make them look like straps, using a hole punch to make three holes.

5 Thread straps through buckles and place on the top of the box, one either side of the handle, using double-sided tape.

6 To make the main strap, cut a length of cardboard to wrap around the suitcase. Cover with the paper and thread through the buckle. Attach to the case with double-sided tape.

7 Tape the foil corners on the front of the suitcase, trimming off the surplus.

8 Haphazardly stick the travel stickers or anything else relevant to the occasion all over the suitcase.

SUGGESTED GIFTS

A needlepoint cushion with the words 'Forget me not'

Waterproof and heavy duty airline bag

Glass paperweight into which a photograph may be sealed

Cotton or linen sachets filled with pot-pourri and tied with ribbon, to be packed into suitcase

HOT STUFF

*S*ince I love breakfast in bed, the message here has to be the ultimate invitation! The design came easily to mind when thinking about this book, but it wasn't the easiest to work on. It took three attempts before I was happy with the bacon, and I still think the egg yolk looks a bit liverish! I should think a real egg looking like this first thing in the morning could almost wreck a romance!

YOU WILL NEED

Any shape of box

Roll of gingham stick-on paper

1 metre (40 in) red ribbon, 1·25 cm (½ in) wide

Shiny red card and black italic pen

Small patty tin, 15 cm (6 in)

50 cm (20 in) black velvet ribbon

Black card for handle of frying pan

Moulding clay—white, yellow, brown and clear varnish

Double-sided tape and scissors

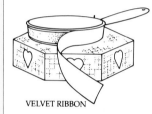

VELVET RIBBON

SUGGESTED GIFTS

A small glass bottle with silver top, filled with a favourite bath oil

A book on leading ladies/men of the cinema

A basket of passion fruit

A copy of the book 'Love is . . .

1 Cover box with gingham paper as shown on page 93.

2 Cut out heart shapes in red, tape to flat sides of box.

3 Cut a larger heart to make the gift tag.

4 Cover the edge of the tin with the ribbon.

5 Cut two long handle shapes out of the black card and stick back to back. Fold over at the base, tape to the tin.

6 First make the clay pliable by rolling in hands. Make a flat thin disc for the egg white; for the egg yolk make a round ball of yellow about 2·5 cm (1 in) and flatten. Use strips of brown and white clay to make the bacon. Varnish the clay.

7 Arrange the 'food' in the bottom of the tin with tape. Tape the tin to the box.

8 Tie ribbons and place around the base of the frying pan. Write the label. Tie to handle, using red ribbon.

make me late for Breakfast x x

MERRY CHRISTMAS FOR NEXT-TO-NOTHING

*T*his was a present I originally made for a friend in a panic on Christmas Eve—a last-minute gift for her assistant. I have re-made it for this book because it shows how useful odd pieces of ribbon and the bits and bobs one collects and keeps can be. Nothing was bought specially—no time! Actually the greenery here was from a gift given to me by Nanette Newman and the red satin ribbon was from an old pantomime costume!

YOU WILL NEED

Any shape of box

Half a sheet of cream leather-look paper

Paper for gift card

Two sprigs of evergreen

1 metre (40 in) tartan ribbon, 2·5 cm (1 in) wide

50 cm (20 in) red satin ribbon, 5 cm (2 in) wide

Cluster of berries and fine wire

Double-sided tape and scissors

Red felt tipped pen

SUGGESTED GIFTS

Comprehensive road atlas

Pair of padded shoe trees

Box of assorted natural soaps

Set of make-up brushes

FIG 1

FIG 2

1 Wrap the box using tuck ends.

2 From the tartan ribbon, cut two lengths of 25 cm (10 in) and put aside.

3 Tie the remaining piece around the box one third of the way up from the bottom, and tie it into a bow.

4 Arrange the spray of evergreen stems under the knot and secure with double-sided tape. See fig 1.

5 Make a bow from the red satin, see page 93. With the wire attach to the tartan knot.

6 With the remaining tartan ribbon tie two bows above and below the large satin bow. See fig 2.

7 Secure berries with wire into centre to hide all the knots.

8 Cut gift card from the paper used and write your message in red ink, then secure with double-sided tape.

A LITTLE EXTRA HELP

I love the unexpected. A gift wrap doesn't always have to mean boxes and paper. This would be perfect to wish a friend happiness in a new home, a present for a green-fingered gardener or for just cheering someone up. You may want to add other trimmings to give your gift a 'fussier' look. Remember, though, whatever you choose, to make sure the colours coordinate.

YOU WILL NEED

50 cm (20 in) of sacking/jute

Needle and cotton

Gardener's raffia twine

Assorted garden tools, seeds, gloves

Pine cones

1 metre (40 in) brown ribbon

Florist wire

Scissors

1 Fold sacking in half, roughly sew up two sides of the sack, turn inside out so that seams do not show.

2 Fill with straw and fold down the top. Arrange the tools on the straw.

3 Plait gardener's twine into a long rope, twist around the tools.

4 Wire fir cones together with florist wire, then attach to the twine plait, adding brown bows. Fish tail the ends of the bows.

SUGGESTED GIFTS

Pack of attractive stationery printed with address

Lovely clematis or climbing rose for the terrace or garden

A bottle of pink champagne to bless the new home

A shrub of the herb rosemary — for remembrance

TICKER-TAPE TREAT

I'm sure you'll want all your gifts to be special but some, perhaps, will be more elaborate than others, requiring extra thought. But gift wrapping for me is a game—I love it, and sometimes I want to pull out all the stops. As with this one—all New York and ticker-tape—it stirs up memories of many happy times spent there. The red, white and blue colours are intense and patriotic and the message quite strong. This is with love to all my friends in New York—I hope they'll agree it has real pizzaz.

YOU WILL NEED

2 metres (80 in) whirly ribbon—I used three colours to match the American flag

Stick-on metallic stars

Cocktail flags

A miniature Statue of Liberty (or, depending on the country, a relevant symbol, eg for France, a miniature Eiffel Tower)

One sheet of wrapping paper

Scissors

Skewer

1 Cover the box with wrapping paper.

2 Cut the whirly ribbon into 30 cm (12 in) lengths and tie them all together by knotting the centre. Curl with scissors (see page 93).

3 Stick knot in the centre of the box, using double-sided tape.

4 Place the Statue of Liberty on top of the knot, using double-sided tape to secure.

5 Make holes with a skewer around the edge of the box and push in the cocktail flags.

(see page 93)

SUGGESTED GIFTS

An Andy Warhol print

A pretty tin of home-made fudge brownies

Stars and Stripes T-shirt

His-and-Hers fun watches

WITH A LITTLE BIT OF LUCK

EASY. TAKES 20 MINUTES

*O*pening nights in the theatre are special, a mixture of excitement, wrecked nerves and hope. It's traditional to exchange gifts—little sillies, nothing too expensive, in case the critics hate you and you find yourself flat on your bottom and out of work by the end of the week! As the words 'Good Luck' are synonymous with black cats I didn't have to think for too long about this design. The only thing I had to go out and buy was the pencil, everything else I had in my old scraps chest. This was a gift for the director, Wendy Toye. Just a loving thought for a treasured friend to bring her luck.

SUGGESTED GIFTS

Leather credit card case

Small folding handbag mirror

Postcards printed with single name and matching envelopes

Travelling sewing kit

YOU WILL NEED

Any shape of box

One-third sheet of white and black cat paper

Double-sided tape

Black knitting wool

Black cat pencil

50 cm (20 in) red satin ribbon, 2·5 cm (1 in) wide

Black felt tipped pen

Scissors

1 Cover the box, using tuck ends.

2 Roll wool into a ball the size of a plum. See figs 1 and 2.

3 Tie red ribbon vertically across the box and tie into a bow.

4 Stick the pencil through one-third of the ball of wool.

5 Place it underneath the bow, using double-sided tape to secure.

6 Cut piece of paper for gift card, 6·5 cm × 6·5 cm ($2\frac{1}{2}$in × $2\frac{1}{2}$in). Fold in half and stick to the box.

FIG 1

WRAP WOOL IN A FIGURE OF EIGHT

FIG 2

MOTHER'S DAY DAZZLER

*T*he talented Kenneth Turner made this jewel tree as a gift for my Mother. She declared it to be a stunning but blatantly extravagant affair and now, of course, it is a treasured possession. Such a colourful but delicate gift should, I feel, be wrapped with nothing but a dream of cellophane and a twist of ribbon, decorated with a few small beads to offset it. Simple, yet so effective.

YOU WILL NEED

The present, which is a plant or dried flower arrangement

25 cm (10 in) moiré taffeta

Small gem stones, colours co-ordinating with the gift and taffeta

Florist wire

50 cm (20 in) ribbon

4 metres (4 yards) cellophane

Double-sided tape

Scissors

Glue for paper

Needle and cotton

1 Stand the gift on a table and liberally cover with the cellophane. It does not matter if it creases.

2 Bunch up at the bottom of the flower pot, using the wire, making the cellophane overlap. Hide the wire with ribbon, secure with tape.

3 Pleat the moire in 1·25 cm ($\frac{1}{2}$ in) pleats, twist into a swirl/bow, attach to the ribbon at the base of the pot with a needle and cotton and double-sided tape. Dot the ribbon with glue and attach gem stones.

SUGGESTED GIFTS

Leather bound recipe book

Set of place card holders

Silver black pepper mill

Pretty nightdress edged with lace

WISHING YOU WELL

*H*ere are two types of designs you could make. The larger box is ideal if you're in a hurry, as it's very easy and quick to do. I slipped a shop-bought squeaker under the paper near the bow, and on the gift card I wrote 'Squeaking of you!'. The round chubby one looks great, doesn't he? I was thrilled when I found the tiny pencil and gushed to the shop assistant 'Oh, I love it ... it's just what I wanted—a perfect thermometer!'. That must have set her thinking as she gave me a very strange look.

YOU WILL NEED

Any shape of box

Half a sheet of white paper

Packet of sticking plasters

50 cm (20 in) white ribbon, 2·5 cm (1 in) wide

One small safety pin

Paper for the gift tag

Double-sided tape

Scissors

1 Cover the box with white paper, using tuck ends.

2 Stick the plasters on in pairs so that they cross over each other.

3 Tie the ribbon around a scroll of paper which is used as the gift tag.

4 Make a bow and attach to the box in the left hand corner using double-sided tape.

5 Thread the safety pin through the paper scroll and bow.

SUGGESTED GIFTS

Little lavender bag to put under the pillow

Tiny teddy-bear for the bedside table

Atomiser of spring water to cool the face

Some quarter bottles of champagne

YOU WILL NEED

One round box

Half a sheet of white wrapping paper

Two buttons for eyes

One different button for the nose

Small black sticky dots

Black felt tipped pen

One very small pencil for a thermometer

50 cm (20 in) red spotted ribbon, 1·25 cm ($\frac{1}{2}$in) wide

Sticking plaster

Glue

Double-sided tape

Scissors

1 Firstly cover the box—see page 93.

2 Using double-sided tape, stick the ribbon around the top rim of the box.

3 Glue the button eyes and nose in position.

4 Draw a downward curve as the mouth; make a hole in the corner of the mouth with the tip of the scissors, slide in the pencil as if it was a thermometer.

5 Add the black dots to make him look ill. (The face can be made female by adding a bow on the head.)

6 Stick a plaster cross on the forehead.

HAPPY BIRTHDAY SWEETIE

*T*his pretty package is all dressed up with netting and sweetie letters, transforming the pink marbled paper into something loving and full of thought. The slice of cake is actually a candle—this might not be the sweetest ever tasted but one slice is definitely enough!

YOU WILL NEED

Any shape of box

Half a sheet of marbled pink wrapping paper

1 candle in the shape of a birthday cake

Sugar initial sweets

Scissors

Double-sided tape

Small amount of pink net

Glue for paper

Needle and cotton

SUGGESTED GIFTS

Needlepoint kit for the beginner

Box of pampering goodies from a natural cosmetic company

Six small white ramekin dishes

Pencil sharpener in leather case

1 Cover the box with wrapping paper, using tuck ends as shown on page 93.

2 Using double-sided tape, secure the candle to the corner of the box.

3 Gather the net, using a draw stitch, and attach to the box so that it lies just behind the candle.

4 Spelling 'Happy Birthday', glue the sugar letters to the box. Pile up the letters on to the back of the cake candle.

I LOVE MY MUSIC

*T*his birthday present makes a wonderful first impression but then the world of music does offer lots of ideas. What makes this effective is the shimmer of the black sequin waste and the gold and silver stars, but make sure you don't spill them all over the floor, as I did. Very annoying—I was like a tiny, mad woman as I scratched around collecting them up. This was for my agent and his wife, Laurie and Mary Evans—their reaction was joyous. No matter how fiddly and time consuming some designs may be, friends' appreciation can be touching. For me there can be no greater pleasure.

YOU WILL NEED

Any shape of box

1 sheet of iridescent paper

Two cake boards (the diameter of the boards should be slightly smaller than the box)

Metallic black card

Adhesive gold and silver stars

Sequin waste

Double-sided tape and scissors

SUGGESTED GIFTS

Concert tickets

Video of a favourite musical show

Pocket-sized radio

Selection of cassette tapes

1 Cover box with wrapping paper, using tuck ends as shown on page 93.

2 Cover one side of the cake boards with the metallic card—see page 92, how to cover a round box.

3 Cut two small circles, using a teacup for a stencil template, out of the iridescent paper—these are to be used as the record labels.

4 Using double-sided tape stick to the centre of the discs. Add a black dot in the centre of each label.

5 Arrange the records on to the top of the box and secure with double-sided tape.

6 Make a sequin waste bow, as shown on page 54. Place bow in the far corner of the box. Scatter and stick the stars all over the box and bow.

BASIC TECHNIQUES

*T*he following techniques have been used in many of the presents featured in this book. These illustrations show the quickest, neatest and simplest ways to cover boxes (especially awkward shaped ones) and foolproof ways to tie ribbons and bows to give a professional finish to any gift.

COVERING A SQUARE BOX

First cover the flat top and tape the overlapping flaps to the sides. Run a long strip of double-sided tape around the sides and cover with a piece of paper cut to the correct depth.

COVERING A FLAT EDGED BOX

Cover the flat top and stick the overlapping flaps to the sides. Remember to angle the corners as shown so the paper lies flat. Cover the sides with a strip of paper, using double-sided tape.

COVERING A ROUND BOX

Cover the top and snip the overlapping paper so that it lies flat against the sides of the box. Cover the sides with a strip of paper, securing with double-sided tape.

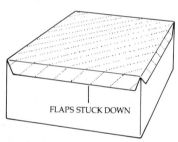

FLAPS STUCK DOWN

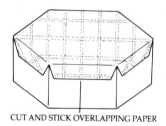

CUT AND STICK OVERLAPPING PAPER

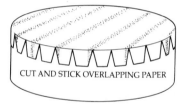

CUT AND STICK OVERLAPPING PAPER

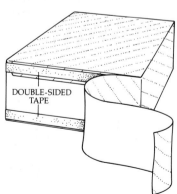

DOUBLE-SIDED TAPE

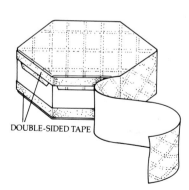

DOUBLE-SIDED TAPE

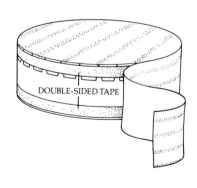

DOUBLE-SIDED TAPE

FOLDING FLAP ENDS

This is one of the easiest ways to cover a box. Firstly, fold down flap 1. Tuck in flaps 2 and 3, folding them into triangles. Fold up flap 4 and secure with double-sided tape.

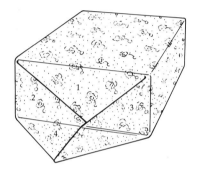

MAKING FISH TAIL ENDS

This gives a decorative finish to bows and prevents the ribbon fraying. Simply fold the ribbon in half lengthways and cut diagonally from the fold line to the outside edge.

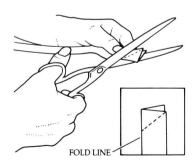

FOLD LINE

MAKING TUCK ENDS

This gives a very neat finish to a box. Wrap the paper around the box and trim the side flaps so that just enough is left to attach the double-sided tape. Fold down the top flap on to the tape as illustrated.

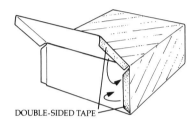

DOUBLE-SIDED TAPE

SHREDDING TISSUE

Fold several sheets together and, using sharp scissors, cut into long, thin strips. This can be used to pack around presents inside boxes to protect them and prevent movement.

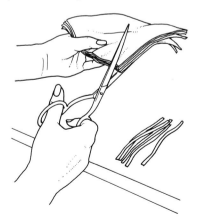

WIRING A BIG BOW

This gives a professional look to bows and prevents them working loose. Fold the ribbon as shown in Fig 1 and secure tightly around the centre with wire. Do not trim the long ends of wire—you can add more bows to them, giving the effect of a large rosette, as in Fig 2.

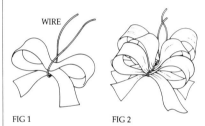

WIRE

FIG 1   FIG 2

MAKING WHIRLY RIBBON

To make ribbon fall into ringlet curls, hold a length of ribbon firmly in one hand. Place the ribbon between the scissor blade and thumb. Pull the blade quickly down the ribbon away from the other hand. Repeat this process until the ribbon has sufficient curls.

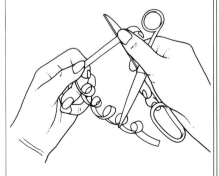

INDEX

The author would like to thank the following suppliers:

The Singing Tree, 69 New Kings Road, London SW6 for the doll's house miniatures on page 41;

Veronica Franklin, 47 Inderwick Road, London N8 for the cushion on page 43 and the Christmas sack on page 53;

Margaret Ballard Originals, Magnum House, 15 Silver Street, Tetbury, Glos for the clay bear on page 61, reproduced by permission of the artist who holds all copyrights and any copyrights coming into existence;

Souleiado, Ltd, 171 Fulham Road, London SW3 for the fabric on page 67;

Edward Marno Flower Shop, 467 Fulham Road, London SW6 for the garden tools on page 79;

Kenneth Turner Flowers, 8 Avery Row, London W1 for the tree on page 85;

Edina Ronay, 141 Kings Road, London SW3 for the clothes worn on the front cover; and Ross at John Frieda.

WEDDING ANNIVERSARIES

Wedding anniversaries are traditionally linked to different fabrics, jewels ... I like to remember this custom when thinking about the wrapping for a gift.

First ◆ Cotton

Second ◆ Paper

Third ◆ Leather

Fourth ◆ Fruit and Flowers

Fifth ◆ Wood

Sixth ◆ Sugar, candy

Seventh ◆ Wool, copper

Eighth ◆ Bronze

Ninth ◆ Pottery, willow

Tenth ◆ Tin

Eleventh ◆ Steel

Twelfth ◆ Silk, linen

Thirteenth ◆ Lace

Fourteenth ◆ Ivory

Fifteenth ◆ Crystal

Twentieth ◆ China

Twenty-fifth ◆ Silver

Thirtieth ◆ Pearl

Thirty-fifth ◆ Coral

Fortieth ◆ Ruby

Forty-fifth ◆ Sapphire

Fiftieth ◆ Gold

Fifty-fifth ◆ Emerald

Sixtieth ◆ Diamond